Colors

Copyright © 1979, Raintree Publishers, Inc.

Library of Congress Number: 79-19116

 3 4 5 6 7 8 9 0 83 82 81

Printed in the United States of America.

Library of Congress Cataloging in Publication Data

Allington, Richard L
  Colors.

  (Beginning to learn about)
  SUMMARY: Simple text and illustrations introduce
12 basic colors and explain how these colors can be
combined to produce other colors.
  1. Color—Juvenile literature. [1. Color]
I. Spangler, Noel. II. Title. III. Series.
QC495.5.A44   535.6   79-19116
ISBN 0-8172-1280-9 lib. bdg.

Richard L. Allington is Associate Professor, Department of Reading,
State University of New York at Albany

BEGINNING TO LEARN ABOUT

COLORS

BY RICHARD L. ALLINGTON, PH. D. • ILLUSTRATED BY NOEL SPANGLER

Raintree Childrens Books • Milwaukee • Toronto • Melbourne • London

The artist draws a picture.
She begins with black.

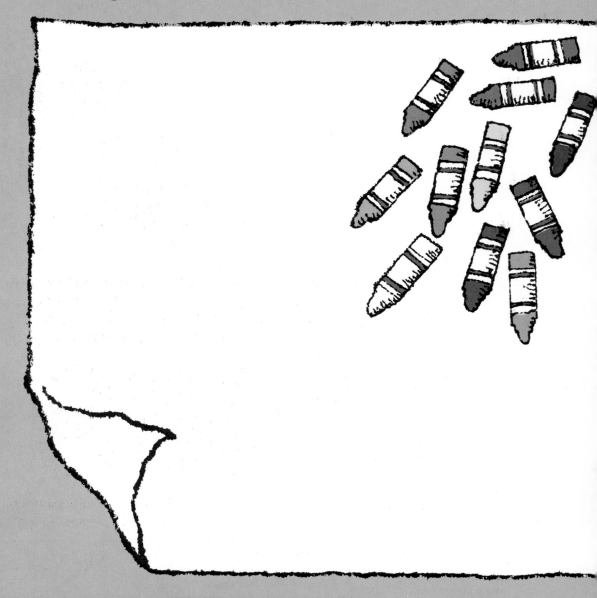

Next she adds red.

APPLE

APPLE

BLUE

Now she adds blue.

BLUEBELLS

APPLE   BLUEBELLS

GRAY

Now she adds gray.

MUSHROOM

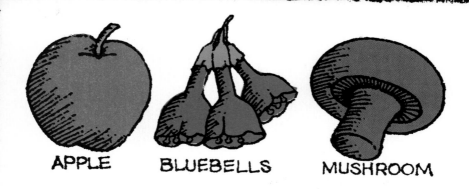

APPLE BLUEBELLS MUSHROOM

PURPLE

Then she adds purple.
Blue and red together make purple.

PLUM

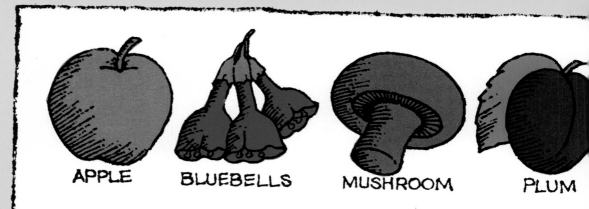

APPLE   BLUEBELLS   MUSHROOM   PLUM

YELLOW

Now she adds yellow.

BANANA

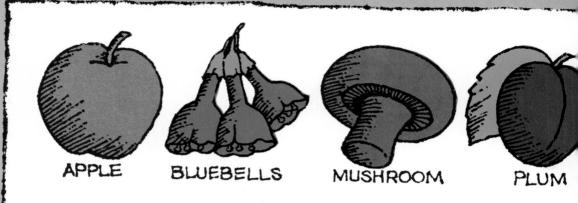

APPLE BLUEBELLS MUSHROOM PLUM

PINK

Next she adds pink.

BANANA

ROSE

17

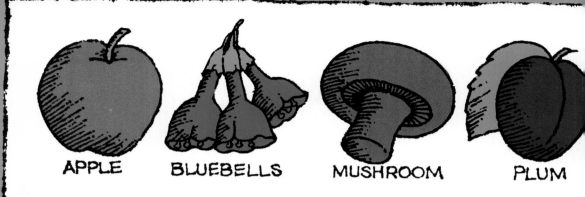

APPLE   BLUEBELLS   MUSHROOM   PLUM

ORANGE

Then she adds orange.
Red and yellow together make orange.

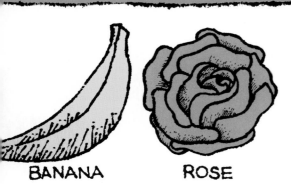

BANANA   ROSE

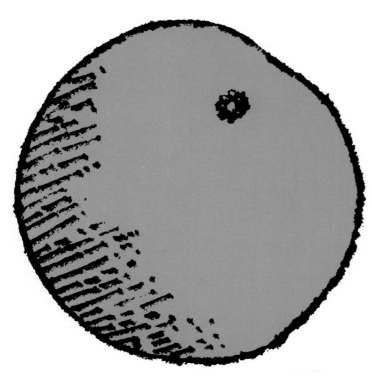

ORANGE

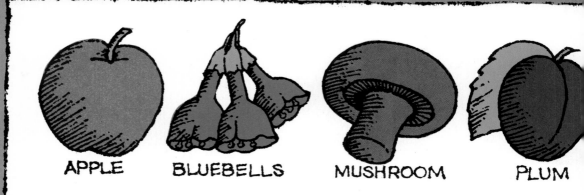

APPLE   BLUEBELLS   MUSHROOM   PLUM

GREEN

Now she adds green.
Blue and yellow together make green.

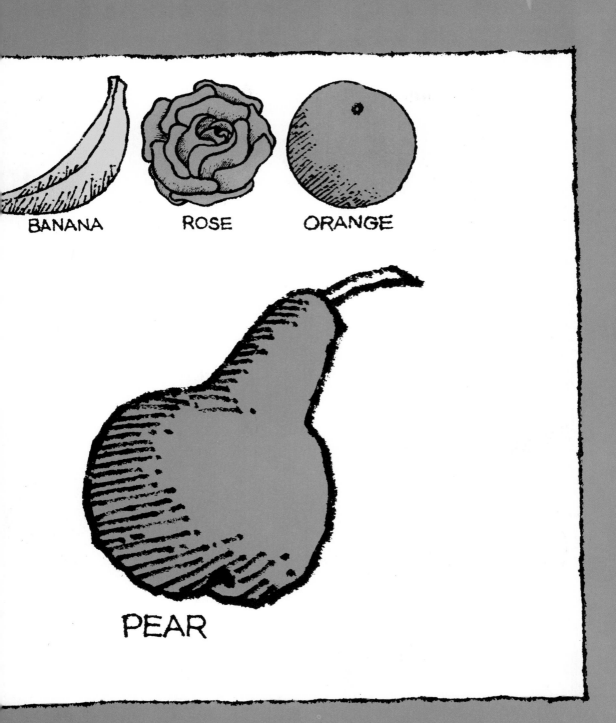

BANANA   ROSE   ORANGE

PEAR

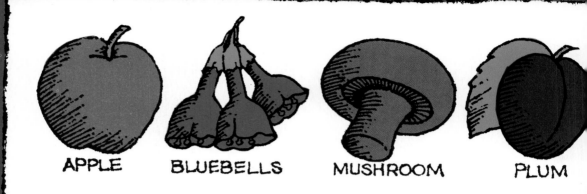

APPLE   BLUEBELLS   MUSHROOM   PLUM

VIOLET

Now she adds violet.

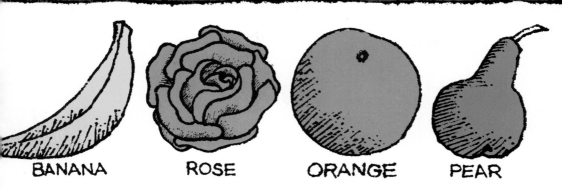

BANANA   ROSE   ORANGE   PEAR

VIOLET

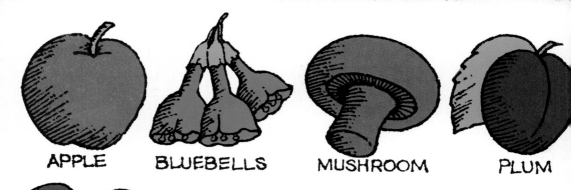

APPLE BLUEBELLS MUSHROOM PLUM

VIOLET

BROWN

Next she adds brown.
Blue and yellow and red make brown.

24

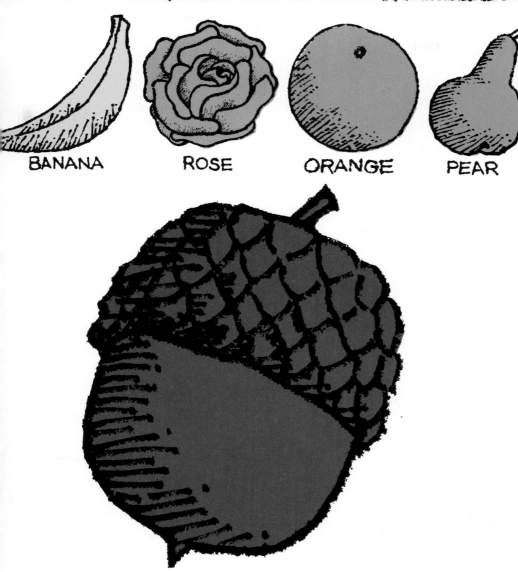

BANANA   ROSE   ORANGE   PEAR

ACORN

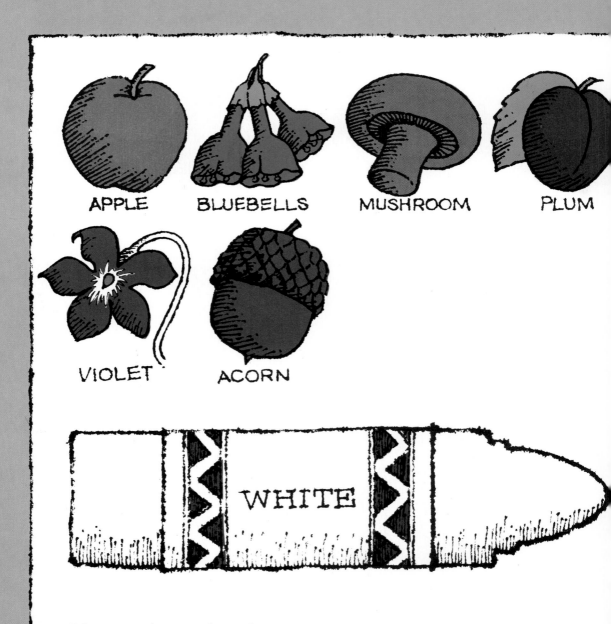

APPLE   BLUEBELLS   MUSHROOM   PLUM

VIOLET   ACORN

WHITE

She ends with white.

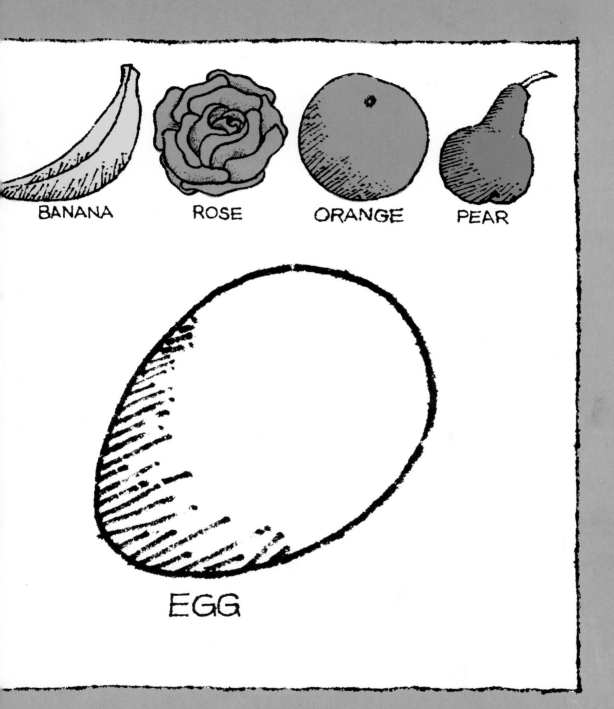

BANANA ROSE ORANGE PEAR

EGG

Now the artist is finished drawing her picture.
Can you name all of the colors in it?

RED

BLUE

GRAY

ORANGE

VIOLET

PINK

The artist puts her new picture on the wall.
What does she call her pictures?

GREEN BLACK WHITE

YELLOW BROWN PURPLE

MY MASTERPIECE

Now the artist puts away her crayons.
Can you name the colors?

With your finger, draw a line from each word to the color that matches.

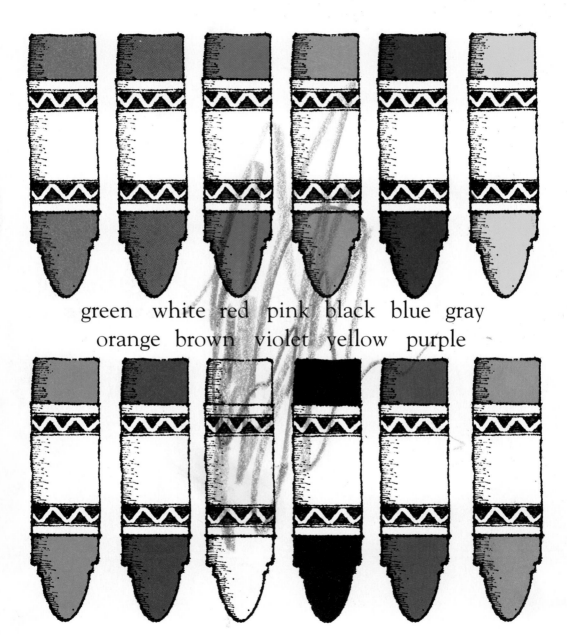

green white red pink black blue gray
orange brown violet yellow purple

Choose your yellow, red, and blue paints.
See how many other colors you can make by mixing them together.